D1154203

Collection Editor: **Jennifer Grünwald**

Assistant Editors: **Alex Starbuck & Nelson Ribeiro**

Editor, Special Projects: **Mark D. Beazley**

Senior Editor, Special Projects: **Jeff Youngquist**

SVP of Print & Digital Publishing Sales: **David Gabriel**

Book Design: **Jeff Powell**

Editor in Chief: **Axel Alonso**

Chief Creative Officer: **Joe Quesada**

Publisher: **Dan Buckley**

Executive Producer: **Alan Fine**

THOR: GOD OF THUNDER VOL. 2 — GODBOMB. Contains material originally published in magazine form as THOR: GOD OF THUNDER #6-11. First printing 2013. ISBN# 978-0-7851-6843-0. Published by MARVEL WORLDWIDE, INC., a subsidiary of MARVEL ENTERTAINMENT, LLC. OFFICE OF PUBLICATION: 135 West 50th Street, New York, NY 10020. Copyright © 2013 Marvel Characters, Inc. All rights reserved. All characters featured in this issue and the distinctive names and likenesses thereof, and all related indicia are trademarks of Marvel Characters, Inc. No similarity between any of the names, characters, persons, and/or institutions in this magazine with those of any living or dead person or institution is intended, and any such similarity which may exist is purely coincidental. **Printed in the U.S.A.** ALAN FINE, EVP - Office of the President, Marvel Worldwide, Inc. and EVP & CMO Marvel Characters B.V.; DAN BUCKLEY, Publisher & President - Print, Animation & Digital Divisions; JOE QUESADA, Chief Creative Officer; TOM BREVOORT, SVP of Publishing; DAVID BOGART, SVP of Operations & Procurement, Publishing; C.B. CEBULSKI, SVP of Creator & Content Development; DAVID GABRIEL, SVP of Print & Digital Publishing Sales; JIM O'KEEFE, VP of Operations & Logistics; DAN CARR, Executive Director of Publishing Technology; SUSAN CRESPI, Editorial Operations Manager; ALEX MORALES, Publishing Operations Manager; STAN LEE, Chairman Emeritus. For information regarding advertising in Marvel Comics or on Marvel.com, please contact Niza Disla, Director of Marvel Partnerships, at ndisla@marvel.com. For Marvel subscription inquiries, please call 800-217-9158. **Manufactured between 8/9/2013 and 9/23/2013 by R.R. DONNELLEY, INC., SALEM, VA, USA.**

10 9 8 7 6 5 4 3 2 1

THOR
GOD OF THUNDER

GODBOMB

WRITER
JASON AARON

ARTIST, #7-11
ESAD RIBIC

PENCILER, #6
BUTCH GUICE

INKER, #6
TOM PALMER

COLOR ARTIST
IVE SVORCINA

LETTERER
VC'S JOE SABINO

COVER ART
ESAD RIBIC

ASSISTANT EDITOR
JAKE THOMAS

EDITOR
LAUREN SANKOVITCH

PREVIOUSLY

In a crusade spanning millennia, a creature known
only as Gorr the God Butcher has vowed to kill
all deities across the cosmos. After numerous
encounters with Thor over the centuries, the God
Butcher has finally revealed the horrific endgame to
his mad quest.

But who is this strange being of deadly reckoning?

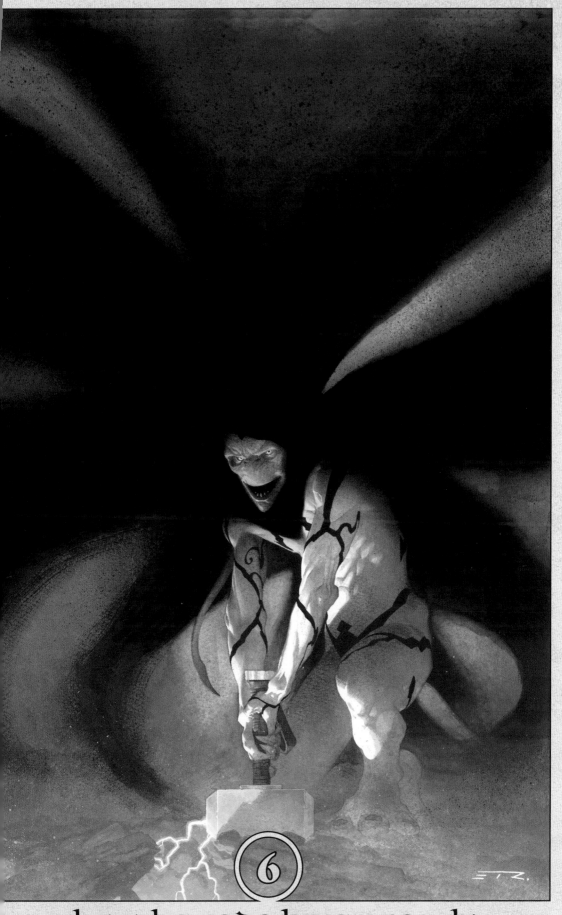

WHAT THE GODS HAVE WROUGHT

I'M SORRY, BUT IT'S ALL I COULD FIND.

HERE, *EAT*.

DON'T WORRY, GORR. THE *NIGHTS* WILL COME SOON. I KNOW IT. THE SKY GODS WILL HEAR OUR PRAYERS AT LAST.

PLEASE, JUST EAT, ARRA. YOU NEED YOUR STRENGTH.

THE *CHILDREN* SLEEP. THOUGH I CAN STILL HEAR THEIR STOMACHS GROWLING.

THIS ONE DOESN'T SLEEP. HE'S GOING TO BE A GREAT HUNTER AND EXPLORER, I CAN TELL. JUST LIKE HIS FATHER.

GREAT HUNTER?

WE'RE *STARVING*, ARRA. THE WHOLE TRIBE.

OUR CAVES ARE EMPTY OF ALL BUT SALT WORMS AND WHAT DAMPNESS WE CAN LICK OFF THE WALLS. WE HAVE TO GO OUT, *SUN* BE DAMNED.

WE HAVE TO LEAVE THE CAVES IF WE'RE GOING TO LIVE.

SHHH, MY LOVE.

THE *GODS* WILL PROVIDE, GORR. *THEY* ALWAYS HAVE.

YOU JUST HAVE TO PUT YOUR LIFE IN THEIR HANDS, MY LOVE. YOU JUST HAVE TO CALM YOURSELF...

AND *LISTEN* FOR THEIR VOICES.

DOES *THAT* ANSWER YOUR QUESTION, LITTLE GOD?

NO.

NO, IT...

I ASKED...IF YOU KNEW WHERE THAT *WEAPON* OF YOURS CAME FROM. BUT YOU DON'T EVEN KNOW THE NAME OF THE GOD YOU STOLE IT FROM, DO YOU?

TO YOU IT'S STILL JUST A...A SHARP STICK FOR POKING THINGS. YOU'RE BLIND TO ITS TRUE--

RRAK!

YOU SPEAK LIKE SOMEONE WHO WOULD RATHER *DIE* THAN BE WHIPPED. TELL ME, WHAT IS YOUR *NAME*, RAGGED WISP OF A GOD?

VOLSTAGG.

I AM...I *WAS*... VOLSTAGG THE VALIANT, LION OF ASGARD.

LET ME ASK *YOU* A QUESTION, VOLSTAGG THE FOOLISH, DOG OF HEAVEN'S DUNG HEAP...

ARRGGHH!

WHAT DO YOU THINK GIVES YOU THE RIGHT TO *STEAL FROM ME?*

IT WAS ONLY A LOAF OF BREAD.

A LOAF OF BREAD THAT WAS NOT YOURS. THIS IS NOT ASGARD, VOLSTAGG THE GREEDY. HERE YOU CANNOT SIMPLY TAKE WHATEVER YOU DESIRE. HERE YOU EAT ONLY WHAT YOU ARE GIVEN.

FOR 500 YEARS SPENT SLAVING IN YOUR MINES I HAVE EATEN NOTHING BUT WORM DROPPINGS AND MY OWN SCABS. EVEN THE MOST FINICKY OF GODS MUST EVENTUALLY GIVE WAY TO HUNGER.

THE SOONER YOU AND YOUR BRETHREN FINISH YOUR WORK, THE SOONER YOUR HUNGER WILL BE SATED. *FOREVER.*

AND TELL ME, GORR THE GOD SLAYER, GORR THE LORD OF SKINFLINTS... WHEN WAS THE LAST TIME *YOU* HUNGERED?

LOOK AT YOURSELF. LOOK AT WHAT THAT WEAPON HAS DONE TO YOU.

YOU'VE BEEN ALIVE FOR THOUSANDS OF YEARS, MURDERING AS YOU PLEASE. YOU'VE RAZED WORLDS AND BUILT YOUR OWN. YOU'VE PUT GODS IN CHAINS.

WHAT ARE YOU, IF NOT A GOD YOURSELF?

THE MOST FOUL AND DESPICABLE GOD I'VE EVER KNOWN.

WHAT? NO MORE WHIPPING? BACK TO EATING WORM POOP IN THE MINES FOR OLD VOLSTAGG, I SUP--

THW**AK**!

ARRRGGHH!!!

7

GODBOMB PART ONE: WHERE GODS GO TO DIE

Iceland, 893 A.D.

IT WAS NOT SO MUCH A SCREAM THAT RANG OUT THROUGH THE VIKING VILLAGE OF KOLKUMÝRAR AS IT WAS A CRY OF BATTLE.

AAAAAAHHHH

THE FIRST OF MANY THAT WOULD BE HEARD THAT NIGHT.

THE NIGHT THE SHADOWS THEMSELVES CAME OUT TO MURDER.

"WHERE IS THE GOD BUTCHER?"

THIS... THIS IS... *HLIDSKJALF.* THE HIGH SEAT OF ODIN.

NO ONE BUT THE *ALL-FATHER* HIMSELF IS ALLOWED IN HERE.

YOU ARE RIGHT ABOUT THAT.

YOU...I MEAN, ME...*WE* ARE THE ALL-FATHER.

I AM THE ALL-FATHER. YOU ARE STILL JUST... WHAT ARE YOU AGAIN?

AN AVENGER? GUARDIAN OF THE GALAXY? THE HEAD OF THAT RIDICULOUS LITTLE *ORDER* OF YOURS?

HAVE YOU MOVED TO THE... AND BECOME COSMIC GOD COP YET?

WHAT? NO.

OH. THEN FORGET I SAID ANYTHING.

WAIT, IF YOU TRULY ARE ME...THEN SHOULDN'T YOU REMEMBER THIS HAPPENING? REMEMBER COMING HERE AND *MEETING* YOURSELF?

I CAN HARDLY REMEMBER HOW TO BUCKLE MY OWN TROUSERS, CAN I? AND THIS IS *TIME TRAVEL* WE'RE TALKING ABOUT. THERE ARE ALL MANNER OF ANNOYING *RULES* GOVERNING THIS SORT OF THING.

I'VE ALWAYS *HATED* TIME TRAVEL.

AND YOU ALWAYS WILL.

WHAT ARE WE LOOKING FOR?

NOW *WHERE WERE WE* WHEN WE LAST MET, BEFORE THOSE VIKING FRIENDS OF YOURS INTERRUPTED US IN THAT CAVE?

Many Millennia From Now, The Black World of Gorr,

"AH YES. I BELIEVE THAT WAS IT.

AYE. THOR IS READY.

BUT I STILL NEED ANSWERS. WHAT HAS HAPPENED TO ASGARD?

GORR THE GOD BUTCHER HAPPENED.

OO YEARS AGO HE CAME HERE UT OF TIME, SPEWING BLACK ERSERKERS. AN ENDLESS ARMY OF THE BEASTS. WE HELD THEM AT BAY AS LONG AS WE COULD.

BUT AS OUR NUMBERS DWINDLED, HIS POWER GREW. AND ULTIMATELY, I WAS ALL THAT WAS LEFT.

HE *KILLED* THEM? HE KILLED *ALL* OF ASGARD?

HE *TOOK* THEM. ENSLAVED THEM.

HE HAS HIS OWN WORLD, A DEAD, BLACKENED PLANET AT THE EDGE OF SPACE. HE'S *BUILDING* SOMETHING THERE, I KNOW NOT WHAT. FOR ALL THESE YEARS, ALL I COULD DO WAS WATCH FROM AFAR.

HE'S KEPT ME TRAPPED HERE, ALONE, FOR NINE CENTURIES. ALWAYS SURROUNDED BY THOSE DAMNED BERSERKERS, UNABLE TO BREAK FREE, UNABLE TO DIE.

I THOUGHT ASGARD WOULD BE MY PRISON FOR ETERNITY.

OR CAN YOU NOT EVEN DO *THAT* CORRECTLY, GOD OF THE WATCH?!

THE COMMUNICATIONS DIVISION HAS TRIED CONTACTING THE WORLD OF *CHRONUX* AS YOU ASKED, LORD LIBRARIAN, BUT WITHOUT SUCCESS.

THE GOD PRIESTS OF THE WORD HAVE DISPATCHED DOZENS OF SPACE RAVENS AND COMET PROBES TO WHERE THEY BELIEVE CHRONUX TO BE HIDDEN, BUT ALL HAVE GONE UNANSWERED.

"WELL? DON'T JUST STAND THERE WASTING MY TIME AND BREATHING MY AIR. *SPEAK!*"

THEY SUGGEST IN THE FUTURE YOU REFRAIN FROM *BURNING* THE BOOKS YOU'VE BEEN ENTRUSTED WITH PROTECTING, ESPECIALLY THOSE CONTAINING THE ONLY KNOWN DIRECTIONS TO HIDDEN WORLDS.

A BILLION GODS IN THIS CITY AND I'M THE ONLY ONE WHO'S NOT AN ABSOLUTE WASTE OF DIVINITY. WHAT ELSE, OH USELESS ONE?

I'VE COMMUNED WITH THE SURVEILLANCE SPIRITS. YOUR LIBRARY WAS THE ONLY DIVISION INFILTRATED. I SUGGEST YOU REVIEW YOUR OWN OBVIOUSLY SUBSTANDARD SECURITY ENCHANTMENTS.

AND WHAT OF THE DEPARTMENT OF *DEATH AND TAXES?* DID YOU GO TO THEM AS I ASKED?

THEIR BLOOD AUDITORS HAVE INDEED REPORTED THE STENCH OF GODBLOOD IN THE CORNER OF THE COSMOS WHERE CHRONUX IS BELIEVED TO BE, BUT THERE IS NO WAY TO--

AND NO WORD FROM THOR?

THE ASGARDIAN? NO, NONE AT ALL.

SKRONK

IF YOU REALLY ARE A GOD, THEN YOUR NAME AND IMAGE ARE SOMEWHERE IN THIS LIBRARY. IF YOU MAKE ME DIG OUT THE BOOK MYSELF, I WILL *BEAT* YOU SENSELESS WITH IT, DO YOU HEAR ME?

IT'S BETTER THIS WAY, I SWEAR! BETTER THAN HOW HE WAS DOING IT!

"TEARING US APART ONE BY ONE! HE MADE ME WATCH! I ONLY HELPED HIM SO I WOULDN'T HAVE TO WATCH ANYMORE, SO *NO ONE* WOULD!"

HE CAME TO ME! HE MADE ME SHOW HIM HOW TO BUILD IT! PLEASE, IT WILL ALL BE BETTER THIS WAY, BELIEVE ME!

START MAKING SENSE, DAMNIT! TELL ME WHAT YOU'RE HIDING! *TELL ME WHO YOU ARE!*

I...

...I AM ONLY SHADRAK. GOD OF...

...GOD OF...

BY ALL *THAT'S* UNHOLY...

8

GODBOMB PART TWO: GOD IN CHAINS

GRRRRGHH!!!

THAT SHALL BE THE LAST TIME YOU EVER *WHIP* AN HEIR TO ASGARD, YOU BLACK-EYED WRETCH!

CARRY THINE OWN DAMN ROCKS!

COME THEN, YOU DOGS OF GORR!

THIS GOD IS NO MAN'S SLAVE!

THE GODS MINED BROKEN MOONS IN SILENCE.

VOICES THAT ONCE SPOKE WHILST GALAXIES OBEYED NOW REDUCED TO FRIGHTENED WHIMPERS AND FEEBLE WEEPING.

KINGS OF HEAVEN AND HELL WHO HAD SAT ATOP OPULENT THRONES NOW SQUATTED IN MUCK AND THEIR OWN FILTH.

THESE WERE GODS IN WHOSE IMAGE GREAT TEMPLES HAD BEEN ERECTED, IN WHOSE NAMES EPIC WARS HAD BEEN WAGED FOR GENERATIONS.

BUT NOW, GLASSY-EYED AND HOLLOW, NOT EVEN THEY COULD REMEMBER WHO THEY WERE.

THAT WILL NEVER BE ME, THOUGHT THE GOD OF THUNDER. NEVER IN A MILLION MILLENNIA WOULD MY SPIRIT BREAK SO UTTERLY.

BUT AT THE SAME TIME, HE THOUGHT IT BEST NOT TO WAIT TOO MANY MILLENNIA TO FIND OUT.

WHAT THE HEL IS THAT THING, THEN?

THOOM

HHGHK

NEVER SPEAK ILL OF MY FATHER. HE IS A *GREAT* MAN. AND YOU ARE BUT A JEALOUS GOD.

OPEN YOUR EYES, BOY. HE ISN'T A *MAN* AT ALL.

NOT ANYMORE.

GET BACK TO WORK, SLAVE.

BEFORE I HAVE YOU CRUCIFIED.

EVERY ONE OF YOU WILL BE *FORGOTTEN!* EVERY GOD EVER SPAWNED! ALL YOUR TEMPLES WILL BE DUST! YOUR HOLY BOOKS BURNED TO ASH!

BUT MY *FATHER'S* NAME WILL NEVER DIE, DO YOU HEAR ME, GODS OF MAN?!

THE NAME OF *GORR THE REDEEMER* WILL LIVE FOREVER!

KING THOR'S SNORING SHOOK THE RIGGING.

GALAXIES PASSED BY IN A BLUR.

THOR THE AVENGER HELD THE GREAT WHEEL STEADY AND CALLED FORTH THE SOLAR STORMS AND ALL THE INTERSTELLAR WINDS HE COULD MUSTER TO PUSH THE FLYING DRAGONSHIP EVER FASTER THROUGH THE COSMIC CURRENTS.

FASTER THAN THE SPEED OF LIGHT OR ALL KNOWN LAWS OF MAN.

FASTER THAN ALL BUT THE BOLDEST OF GODS HAD EVER DARED.

HE TALKED TO HIS HAMMER AS HE SAILED, CHASING THE STENCH OF DEAD GODS ACROSS THE SPACEWAYS.

HE STRUGGLED TO PUT DOUBTS FROM HIS MIND. WORRIES THAT BURIED WITHIN GORR'S VENGEFUL RANTS...THERE WAS SOME SMALL EMBER OF TRUTH.

A TRUTH THAT THREATENED TO CONSUME HIM.

THOR SAILED ON, CRAVING COMBAT WITH EVERY OUNCE OF HIS BEING.

COMBAT, AND JUST A BIT MORE ALE.

I'M YOUR GOD.

THE EUNUCH? WHO LET HIM IN?

NO OFFENSE, FRIEND, BUT WE DON'T EVEN KNOW WHO YOU ARE.

I AM THE FAVORITE SON OF ODIN, THE OMNIPOTENT. HEIR TO THE THRONE OF ETERNAL ASGARD. THE LORD OF THE STORM AND GOD OF THE THUNDER. HIM BEFORE WHOM EVEN VIKINGS BOW.

THEY CALL M THOR.

THOR? OH MY HEAVENS... I'VE BEEN HAVING IMPURE THOUGHTS ABOUT MY GRANDFATHER.

GORR HAS BEEN KNOWN TO PULL GODS OUT OF THE TIMESTREAM. BUT IF YOU'RE REALLY WHO YOU SAY, THEN YOU SHOULD HAVE NO TROUBLE SUMMONING A THUNDERSTORM TO COVER OUR ATTACK.

BEH. HE'S NO THOR. WE'RE THE GODDESSES OF THUNDE AND EVEN WE CAN'T SUMMON STORMS I THIS MISERABLE DUNGHOLE.

I'VE TRIED, BUT...THIS WORLD IS TOO BARREN.

THERE ARE NO STORMS HERE THAT ANSWER THOR'S CALL.

DON'T FEEL TOO BAD. HAINT, THE RAIN GOD, CAN'T EVEN MAKE IT DEW ANYMORE. AND GORD, THE WINE LORD, CAN ONLY TURN WATER INTO VINEGAR.

WE NEED MORE WEAPONS IF WE'RE GOING TO CROSS THE BLACK PLAIN AND REACH THAT BOMB. CLUBS, SHARP STONES, WHATEVER WE CAN FIND.

THIS BOMB... CAN IT REALLY KILL ALL THE GODS?

...RR HAS PROVEN HIMSELF TO BE MANY THINGS, BUT A *LIAR* ISN'T ONE OF THEM.

THEN WHAT IS YOUR PLAN?

TO DESTROY THE BOMB BEFORE IT'S FINISHED.

THAT THING IS THE SIZE OF A *MOON*. HOW DO YOU EXPECT TO DESTROY IT WITH A FEW RAGGED SLAVES ARMED WITH CLUBS AND SHARP STONES?

FOR 900 YEARS, WE "RAGGED SLAVES" HAVE MINED THE CORES OF DEAD STARS AND BROKEN PLANETS, BUILDING GORR'S GODBOMB.

THIS IS EVERY SCRAP OF UNSTABLE MATTER WE'VE BEEN ABLE TO STEAL AND HIDE OVER THE YEARS.

HE'S GOT HIS BOMB. WE'VE GOT *OURS*.

BUT THE QUESTION STILL REMAINS, HOW DO WE GET CLOSE ENOUGH TO THE GODBOMB TO DESTROY IT WITHOUT BEING HARMED BY BLACK BERSERKERS?

WE RUSH THEM. EVERY GOD WHO CAN WALK. ALL AT ONCE.

IT WON'T WORK. GORR'S WEAPON IS TOO STRONG. HIS BERSERKERS ARE EVERYWHERE.

THEN WE SNEAK OUR BOMB AS CLOSE AS WE CAN AND DETONATE IT BY HAND.

THAT'S SUICIDE.

THAT'S THE ONLY WAY. ONE GOD MUST DIE FOR THE REST TO SURVIVE.

THEN LET'S SEE A SHOW OF HANDS. WHICH GOD WILL VOLUNTEER TO...

OH YOU STUPID, STUPID THOR.

IN ORBIT AROUND GORR'S WORLD,
STARSHARKS FEED ON THE FLESH
OF DEAD GODS, CAST INTO THE
VOID OVER THE CENTURIES.

BEST
FETCH YOUR
HAMMER, BOY. I SENSE
SOMETHING STIRRING.
SOMETHING CLOSE.
SOMETHING...

...STRANGELY
FAMILIAR.

IS THAT...?

YES, LUCKY ME. *ANOTHER* ONE.

WHO ARE YOU GRIZZLED OLD BASTARDS AND WHAT IS YOUR BUSINESS HERE? IF YOU BE *SLAVE TRADERS*, YOU WILL ANSWER THIS DAY TO...

...TO...

... *FATHER*? IS THAT *YOU*?

BOR'S *BONES*. ARE YOU *CERTAIN* THERE ISN'T ANY ALE LEFT?

OON.

YOU SURE YOU'RE UP FOR THIS? YOU JUST ESCAPED FROM GORR'S SLAVE WORLD, AND NOW YOU'RE ABOUT TO GO MARCHING RIGHT BACK IN.

IF YOU TWO OLD FARTS ARE UP FOR IT, THEN I GUESS THAT MEANS I AM AS WELL, DOESN'T IT?

BLASTED *TIME TRAVEL*. WHO EVER KNEW THERE WAS SUCH A THING?

THEN *ARM* YOURSELF, BOY. AND BE QUICK ABOUT IT.

9

GODBOMD PART THREE: THUNDER IN THE BLOOD

Moments Later,
Light-Years Away.

SUCH WAS THE AWESOME
MIGHT OF AN ALL-FATHER
UNLEASHED, THAT FOR THE
FIRST TIME IN MILLENNIA...

THE BUTCHER OF
GODS KNEW FEAR.

THE TRUE HISTORY OF GORR'S WEAPON HAD BEEN LOST TO TIME, THOUGH THERE WERE MANY DIFFERENT STORIES AND LEGENDS.

SOME SAID IT WAS A BLADE FORGED BY THE ELDER GODS AND USED IN THE TIME OF CREATION TO CARVE EXISTENCE FROM THE UNBREAKABLE STONE OF NOTHINGNESS.

OTHERS SAID IT WAS THE DARKNESS IN ALL GODS GIVEN FORM, AND THAT WHOEVER WIELDED IT WAS MERELY AN EMPTY VESSEL FOR ITS MURDEROUS WILL.

THERE WERE STORIES THAT IT HAD SLAIN BILLIONS UPON BILLIONS EVEN BEFORE GORR. THAT IT HAD RAGED THROUGH WORLDS LIKE A WILDFIRE THROUGH DRY STALKS.

THAT ITS POWER WOULD CONTINUE TO GROW FOR ALL TIME, UNTIL THE DAY IT FINALLY BLACKENED ALL OF INFINITY.

PERHAPS ON THAT DAY THEY WILL TELL STORIES OF THIS ONE.

OF THE DAY GORR'S BLACK WORLD BECAME RINGED WITH BLOOD AND THE SCREAMING OF GODS FILLED THE COSMOS ENTIRE.

THE DAY THE LORDS OF ALL THE HEAVENS WERE SLAUGHTERED LIKE LAMBS.

COME! I NEVER GET TIRED OF KILLING THORS!

WITH EVERY SWING OF HIS MIGHTY HAMMER, THOR FELT HIS BONES RATTLE. HIS FINGERS CRACK. HIS MUSCLES TEAR.

AND YET, HE SWUNG AGAIN. EVEN HARDER THAN BEFORE.

AND AGAIN.

AND AGAIN.

WITH EVERY CUT, HE FELT GORR'S WEAPON CREEP INSIDE HIM, BURROWING DEEPER INTO HIS FLESH. BROKEN BLADES BECAME BLACK MAGGOTS, EATING HIM FROM THE INSIDE.

BUT THOR MADE HIS MIND AS HARD AS THE URU OF HIS HAMMER, AND HE THUNDERED ON.

THOR IGNORED THE PAIN. THE ROAR OF HIS OWN SCREAMS. THE SHATTERING OF WORLDS AROUND HIM.

THOR FOCUSED ONLY ON BLUDGEONING AND IGNORED...

...EVERYTHING... ELSE.

NO. THAT'S NO EMPTY MOON.

SOMEWHERE IN THE COSMOS, STARWHALES BEACHED THEMSELVES ON AN ASTEROID AND DIED, HUNDREDS OF THEM, FOR SEEMINGLY NO REASON AT ALL.

A DOG WAS BORN WITH THE FACE OF A CHILD, SCREAMING IN TERROR. IT DID NOT LIVE FOR LONG.

A SAINTLY WOMAN DIED AND FOUND NO ONE WAITING FOR HER ON THE OTHER SIDE, NO WHITE LIGHT TO GUIDE HER, NOTHING.

THE SACRED WATERS OF THE WELL OF MIMIR TURNED RED AND BITTER.

THE WORLD TREE BLED AT THE ROOTS.

IN ASGARD, THE STATUES OF THE KINGS BEGAN WEEPING.

AND ON A BACKWOODS WORLD, AN ALIEN BOY LOOKED UP AT THE MORNING SKY...

AND SAW THE SUN TURN BLACK.

AR

On the world of Gorr, thunder is heard. And then it began to rain.

RRRRRUMBLE

It rained blood.

Godblood.

THOOM THOOM THOOM

Then it rained HAMMERS.

⑩

GODBOMB PART FOUR: TO THE LAST GOD

... THE WORLD OF THE SLAUGHTERED
... SLAVES, THE GROUND OPENED
... A GREAT BLACK MAW, AND
... OR THE AVENGER FELL.

MJOLNIRS LAY ENCASED
IN A CAGE OF GODFLESH,
UNABLE TO FLY TO THEIR
MASTERS' HANDS.

AND YOUNG THOR FOUND
HIMSELF TOO SPENT TO
EVEN MUSTER A CURSE...

FATHER, IS IT TRUE?

IS IT TIME TO TRIGGER THE BOMB?

IT...IT IS INDEED.

WHERE'S MOTHER?

SHE SAID SHE WAS COMING TO MEET YOU. SHE SHOULD BE HERE TO SEE THIS.

LOOK FOR HER IN THE TOWERS, BOY. BUT DON'T EXPECT ME TO WAIT.

I HAVE TOO MANY GODS TO KILL.

YES, FATHER.

AND OF COURSE WE MUST MAKE SURE...

...WE KILL THEM ALL.

LOOK AT IT. *BEAUTIFUL,* ISN'T IT?

IT WAS DESIGNED BY A GOD NAMED *SHADRAK.* OF THE DIAMOND MOONS OF OGHOGHO. THE GOD OF BOMBS AND FIREBALLS.

HE ENJOYED CASTING THEM INTO SPACE, SO HE AND HIS FRIENDS COULD WATCH THE STARS EXPLODE.

AFTER JUST ONE AFTERNOON OF WATCHING HIS *FRIENDS* EXPLODE, HE BEGGED ME TO LET HIM BUILD THIS.

IT TOOK *900* YEARS AND AN ARMY OF *GOD SLAVES* TO BRING SHADRAK'S DESIGNS TO LIFE.

IT WAS BUILT AROUND THE HEART OF AN ELDER GOD, AND INFUSED WITH THE CHRONOMANCY OF THE TIME LORDS OF CHRONUX. AND ONCE I TRIGGER IT...

...WITH *THIS...*

...IT WILL EXPLODE THROUGH TIME. KILLING EVERY GOD WHO EVER LIVED.

OR EVER WILL.

AMEN.

WHAM

POP

RRUUMN BLE

WHAT THE...WE'RE NOT DEAD.

GAHH. BITING YOUR TONGUE HURTS LIKE HEL.

LOOK! WEAPONS!

ARM YOURSELVES! THIS DAY WE'RE SLAVES NO MORE!

TODAY WE DIE LIKE GODS!

STUPID HAMMER. MUST BE BROKEN. WON'T BUDGE...

HEY!

KROOOM

THE GODBOMB SEETHED WITH POWER.

THE ROARING OF THE MJOLNIRS SHOOK THE STARS.

THOR FOUGHT TO CHOKE DOWN FEAR. BUT IT BUBBLED UP LIKE BILE.

AND GORR'S WORDS BURROWED DEEP INT HIS MARROW.

WHAT IF THEY REALLY ARE BETTER OFF WITHOUT US, THOR WONDERED IN FEAR.

HA HA HA.

EVEN AS HE SWUNG HIS HAMMERS.

WHAT IF A GODLESS AGE IS WHAT THEY DESERVE?

WHAT IF GORR... ISN'T A MADMAN AT ALL?

GODS HELP US, WHAT IF HE'S...

11

GODBOMB PART FIVE: THE LAST PRAYER

In the Far Future,
The World of the Godbomb,

AAAAAHHH!!!

UUUUGGHH!!!

RRRRRRRGGHH!!!

YOU'RE DYING.

AND YOU KNOW IT. DON'T YOU, KING THOR?

DYING OVER EVERY SECOND OF YOUR LIFE ALL AT ONCE. YOU AND TRILLIONS MORE JUST LIKE YOU.

I DO HOPE IT HURTS.

*I*NSIDE THE HEART OF THE GODBOMB, TIME BECAME TAR.

*E*TERNITY ECHOED WITH WAILING AND THE GNASHING OF TEETH. WITH THE DYING OF THE GODS.

GGGRRRAAEEGHHH!!!

IF HE'D BEEN A LESSER GOD, THOR MIGHT HAVE ACCEPTED THAT GORR HAD WON. AND MORE SO, THAT GORR DESERVED TO WIN.

THAT GODS WERE CRUEL AND JEALOUS CREATURES. THAT IT WAS TIME FOR THEIR AGE TO PASS.

BUT THIS WAS NO LESSER GOD

THIS WAS THE GOD OF ROARING THUNDER AND RAGING STORMS, AND EVEN IF HE HAD BEEN THE LAST GOD LEFT ALIVE IN ALL THE UNIVERSE...

SHA

TUNNG

HE STILL WOULD HAVE BEEN GOD ENOUGH.

HHHHRRRRGEHH!!

WHAT...IS HE DOING?

DYING. LIKE A GOD.

ALL THROUGH TIME, GODS WERE DYING.

EVERY GOD WHO HAD EVER BEEN BORN OR EVER WOULD BE.

THERE WAS NO FINAL BATTLE FOR THEM TO FIGHT. NO ENEMIES STANDING OVER THEM. NO WARNING EVEN.

THEY MERELY FELL TO THEIR KNEES, CHOKING ON BLACKNESS, THEIR FLESH FALLING APART BEFORE THEIR EYES.

SOME KNEW WHY IT WAS HAPPENING. MOST DID NOT. BUT IN THEIR FINAL CLOUDY MOMENTS, THEY ALL SHARED A COMMON VISION.

A VISION OF ONE GOD, WITH A MIGHTY HAMMER IN EACH HAND, FIGHTING AT THE HEART OF A BOMB TO SAVE THEM ALL.

AND FOR ONE MOMENT THAT STRETCHED ACROSS TIME...

...EVERY GOD IN ALL THE UNIVERSE CLOSED THEIR EYES...

AND PRAYED TO THOR.

I'D HAD ABOUT ENOUGH OF THAT.

THUS ENDETH THE TALE OF THE GOD BUTCHER.

SHALL WE DRINK MEAD AND THINK OF WAYS TO DEFILE HIS ASHES?

BBLAAAAUURRGGHH

THE WEAPON IS STILL INSIDE YOU. HURRY. YOU MUST PURGE YOURSELF.

TOO LATE. JUST MAKE CERTAIN...

THAT YOU PROVE HIM WRONG.

THUS DIED THOR.

FOR THE NINTH TIME THAT COULD BE REMEMBERED.

THE THORS WOULD NOT REMEMBER HAVING MET THEMSELVES. AND CHANCES WERE, THEY WOULD NEVER MEET AGAIN IN SUCH A WAY.

INSTEAD THEY RETURNED TO THEIR OWN SEPARATE WORLDS AND LIVES.

THEIR OWN AMBITIONS.

THEIR OWN FEARS.

THEIR OWN CALLINGS.

AND ALSO, THEIR ONE COMMON DESTINY...

TO BE THE GREATEST GOD WHO EVER LIVED.

Next: Thor Returns to Midgard.

#7 MANY ARMORS OF IRON MAN VARIANT
BY GABRIELE DELL'OTTO

#6, PAGE 19 PENCILS & INKS
BY BUTCH GUICE & TOM PALMER

#6, PAGE 20 PENCILS & INKS
BY BUTCH GUICE & TOM PALMER

TO ACCESS THE FREE *MARVEL AUGMENTED REALITY APP*
THAT ENHANCES AND CHANGES THE WAY YOU EXPERIENCE COMIC

1. Download the app for free via
   marvel.com/ARapp
2. Launch the app on your camera-enabled
   Apple iOS® or Android™ device*

3. Hold your mobile device's camera ov
   any cover or panel with the **AR** grap
4. Sit back and see the future of comics
   in action!

*Available on most camera-enabled Apple iOS® and Android™ devices. Content subject to change and availability.

THOR: GOD OF THUNDER INDEX